W9-CLB-729

DISCARD

Scorpions

DISCARD

DISCARD

SCORPIONS

Charlene W. Billings

*Illustrated with photographs
and diagrams*

DODD, MEAD & COMPANY
New York

A SKYLIGHT BOOK

12/83 WLS 7⁹⁵

J
595.4
B

45255

ACKNOWLEDGMENTS

The author wishes to acknowledge the invaluable assistance of those who have provided information and photographs for this book. Special thanks to Dr. Clifford S. Crawford of the University of New Mexico and Steven J. Prchal for answering questions, identifying species, and taking photographs for the book.

ILLUSTRATION CREDITS

Arizona-Sonora Desert Museum, 15, 20, 24, 33, 34, 38, 39, 42; Armed Forces Institute of Pathology, 43; C.S. Crawford, 30, 31; Florida Department of Agriculture, 37; Johan Kooy, Art Director, Pacific Discovery, California Academy of Sciences, 11, 12; Steven J. Prchal, 8, 13, 16, 23, 44; E.S. Ross, 40; D.D. Tyler, 28; and U.S. Department of Health, Education, and Welfare, 21, 25.

Text copyright © 1983 by Charlene W. Billings
Drawing on page 28 copyright © 1983 by D. D. Tyler
All rights reserved
No part of this book may be reproduced in any form
without permission in writing from the publisher
Printed in the United States of America

1   2   3   4   5   6   7   8   9   10

Library of Congress Cataloging in Publication Data

Billings, Charlene W.
  Scorpions.

  (A Skylight book)
  Includes index.
  Summary: Discusses members of the order Scorpionida,
the lobster-shaped venomous arachnids that thrive the
world over, including their physiology, life cycle, habits,
and behavior.
  1. Scorpions—Juvenile literature. [1. Scorpions]
I. Title.
QL458.7.B54   1983   595.4′6   82–45994
ISBN 0-396-08125-8

For Barry

Contents

Giant hairy scorpion (Hadrurus sp.) eating a cricket.

1

Scorpions and People

The chirping cricket is unaware of danger nearby.

Without warning, the giant hairy scorpion seizes the prey with its large claws. It flashes the poisonous tip of its tail forward to sting the struggling insect. The lightning attack silences the cricket's song and the scorpion eats its freshly caught supper.

This is how scorpions normally use their poison—to capture food. They also use the poison to defend themselves from their natural enemies.

Unfortunately, scorpions sometimes sting people too. These animals are not aggressive toward humans. When they sting a person, it is usually because they have been disturbed suddenly or accidentally annoyed.

9

A scorpion's poison or venom is a liquid which injures or destroys the soft body parts or nervous system of its victim. Popular belief is that the sting of a scorpion means certain death, but only some species have poison strong enough to kill an adult man or woman. Nevertheless, throughout the world many people fear all scorpions, just as they are afraid of snakes and spiders.

In the United States, the venom of most of our forty or so species of scorpions is not deadly to humans. A sting from these scorpions is much like that of a bee or wasp, painful, but not a real threat to life. Only the sculptured scorpion (*Centruroides sculpturatus*) from our Southwest can cause death.

However, in India, Pakistan, and countries in the dry areas of North Africa, the large number of deaths caused by scorpions is a serious medical problem. In Mexico, even in recent years, as many as one thousand people die annually from the sting of these animals. This is many times the number of deaths caused by snakebite. Most of the fatalities are young children who are affected more by the venom because they weigh less than an adult. So, the

The Egyptian Goddess Selquet.

human fear of scorpions is not entirely unfounded.

To ancient man, scorpions were mystical creatures with supernatural powers which they both feared and honored. For this reason, scorpions have become part of our legends and myths. The Egyptians of long ago had a scorpion-goddess, Selquet, who wore the animal sacred to her on her head. Sometimes she also was pictured as a scorpion with a woman's head.

According to Greek fable, Orion, the hunter, boasted that he could kill any animal on earth. As punishment for

Constellation Scorpius.

his self-pride, the goddesses Diana and Latona sent a scorpion to sting Orion to death. The scorpion later was raised to heaven where it became a constellation of the Zodiac. On summer nights in North America you can see the group of stars we still know as Scorpius.

Often, scorpions are called living fossils because their appearance has changed little in over 350 million years. In

The Imperial scorpion, Pandinus imperator—*the largest scorpion known living today.*

the past some scorpions were giants. Proof of this is a fossil from Scotland (*Gigantoscorpio*) which is sixteen inches long. This is twice as big as any scorpion now alive. Today, the largest scorpion is an eight-inch species which lives in Guinea, on the west coast of Africa. In contrast, the smallest scorpion measures only one-half inch in length.

13

2

Where Do Scorpions Belong in the Animal Kingdom?

Spiders, mites, and harvestmen, which we also call daddy longlegs, are relatives of scorpions. In the scientific scheme of things, all belong to the class Arachnida. Unlike insects, arachnids are wingless and have eight legs instead of six.

The order Scorpionida is made up of six families, which include all of the 700 or more kinds of scorpions known in the world. Five families of scorpions have members which live in the United States. The only areas of our country where scorpions have not been found are New England and the states surrounding the Great Lakes.

The largest family of scorpions, the Buthidae, has over 300 species worldwide. It is most important because it con-

14

This jumping spider is related to the scorpion.

tains all of the scorpions which are dangerous to man. Within this family is the genus *Centruroides* which has several deadly species.

The giant hairy scorpions and species commonly called devil scorpions are frequently seen in the United States. These belong to another well-known family, the Vejovidae.

The three remaining families represented in the United States are less numerous, and only the Diplocentridae are seen very often.

Although most scorpions live in warm regions of the earth, they are surprisingly widespread. In the Northern Hemisphere, one species lives as far north as Alberta, Canada. Scorpions also are found in Mongolia and Asia. In Europe, Germany and France have scorpions as residents. In the Southern Hemisphere, only the Antarctic, New Zealand, the southern part of Argentina and Chile are without scorpions.

Scorpions thrive in a variety of climates and conditions. Some live as high as 6,000 feet in the European Alps and a

Giant hairy scorpion.

South American species up to 16,000 feet in the Andes. Scorpions also prosper beneath the bark of palm trees in tropical jungles and rain forests, in burrows they dig in dry sandy deserts, and even under rocks in places where snow is plentiful in winter.

For the most part, scorpions live solitary lives and will not allow others to be nearby. Individuals try to avoid each other. If they cannot, they often fight to the death. The victor then devours the victim. However, there are exceptions. Common stripe-back scorpions can be discovered stacked like flapjacks, filling the spaces in rotting logs, especially in periods of drought or during winter. The same is true for the sculptured scorpion.

3

A Closer Look at Scorpions

A scorpion looks a bit like a small lobster. It has a tough, leathery skeleton on the outside of its body for protection. Scattered over the surface of this *exoskeleton* (exo- means outside) are many fine hairs which can detect vibrations in the air and are sensitive to touch.

From time to time a scorpion must shed or molt its confining covering in order to grow to full size. First, a new skeleton begins to form under the old one and, eventually, the outer covering splits and is cast aside. For a few hours the soft-shelled scorpion bends, stretches, and actively grows before its new skeleton hardens. During this time the scorpion is defenseless and so stays out of sight.

If a scorpion loses a leg in a fight, a new one starts to

The scorpion looks like a small lobster.

grow. After two or three molts the replacement limb catches up to the length of the other legs.

Like most arachnids, a scorpion has two major parts to its body. The front end is the *cephalothorax*, which consists of the combined head and trunk of the body. The back part is the *abdomen*.

20

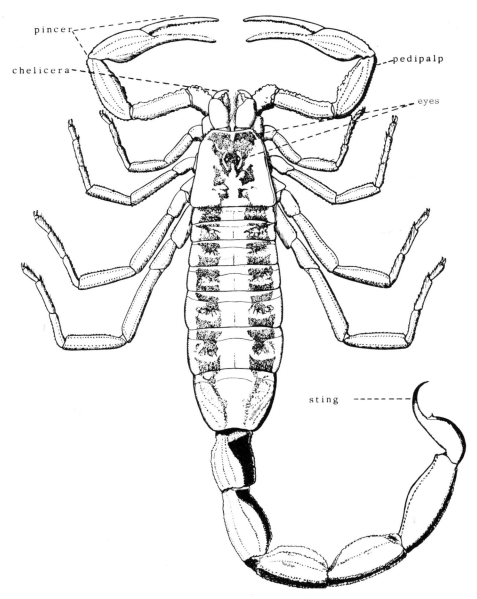

pincer

chelicera

pedipalp

eyes

sting

Scorpion diagram—dorsal view.

A hard shield-shaped piece covers the front portion of the body. On the shield are one pair of eyes near the center and two clusters of two to five small eyes near the front edges. The number of small eyes depends upon the species. But having as many as a dozen eyes does not mean that scorpions see well. In fact, all they can do is tell light from dark. However, scorpions are creatures which shun daylight and hunt mostly at night.

In front of the opening to the mouth is a pair of small pincers or *chelicerae* (key-lis'-er-ee). These pincers crush, cut, and tear food into shreds and push it toward the mouth.

The scorpion's noticeably large clawed arms are the *pedipalps*. These are attached to the cephalothorax at either side of the mouth. On these arms are a second kind of highly sensitive hair. Each of these hairs is set into a shallow dimple. A thin sheet, which looks like the top of a tiny toy drum, surrounds the base of each hair. These hairs detect and magnify vibrations in the air so that they serve as miniature antennas or "ears." The arms are moved to tune in on the source of any disturbance.

Scorpions do not have voices, but some species make

Close-up of the chelicerae of a giant hairy scorpion.

noises to try to scare away predators when threatened. One kind, which lives in southern India, has a scraper on each of its pedipalps and a rasp on each of its first pair of legs. By rubbing scraper against rasp, a sound similar to running your finger along a fine-toothed comb is made.

Four pairs of walking legs attached to the trunk have small claws at their tips.

The abdomen is made up of twelve sections or segments. The first seven of these are wide. The last five segments are narrow and form the part commonly called the tail.

Tooth-like spur on the stinger of the deadly sculptured scorpion.

Attached to the last segment of the abdomen is the sting. It contains a pair of venom-filled glands and is equipped with a needle-sharp, curved barb to inject the poison. The deadly sculptured scorpion of Arizona has a toothlike spur on its stinger as well. Though some other species in the United States have this feature, none of them live within the state of Arizona.

Once in a while a scorpion is born with a double tail. This rare abnormality happens when an animal does not complete development into twins. Imagine how extraordinary such a scorpion must have seemed to superstitious people of long ago!

Several structures on the underside of the broad abdominal segments are easy to see. The most obvious are a pair

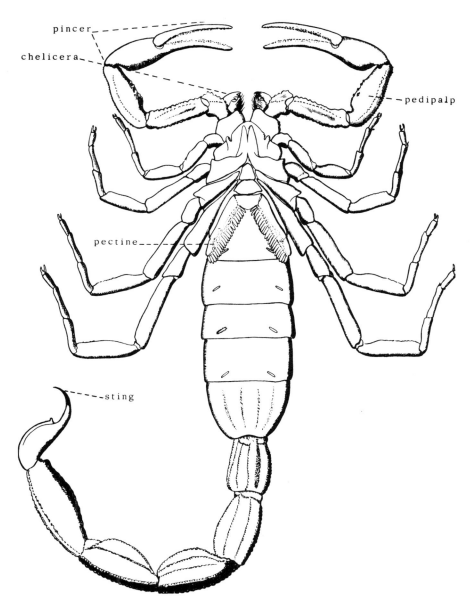

pincer

chelicera

pedipalp

pectine

sting

Scorpion diagram—ventral view.

of combs known as *pectines*. These are found only on scorpions and on no other creatures in the animal kingdom. Each comb may have from three to forty teeth along its edge. The number varies from one species to another. The pectines are richly supplied with nerves which react to touch, vibrations, and possibly odors. Some scientists think that scorpions use them to feel their way through the darkness of night.

Near the base of the pectines is the *genital opening*. Through this opening the male gives off sperm and the female gives birth to her young.

Segments three, four, five, and six each have a pair of *book lungs* by which scorpions breathe. Each book lung has many paper-thin folds—arranged like the pages of a book—where oxygen and carbon dioxide are exchanged. Air enters and leaves the book lungs through paired openings called *spiracles*. The spiracles are the two slits you see on either side of each of the segments.

Scorpions do not seem to need much oxygen. Amazingly, they can live even with seven of their eight spiracles blocked and have been known to revive after being under water for several hours.

4

Courtship—the Dance of Death

A male scorpion approaches a female with great care when courting. To be mistaken for an enemy could be fatal. If the female accepts him, the male grasps her large claws with his own and the couple may spend hours parading back and forth holding "hands." This strange wedding dance has been called "the dance of death," since the male sometimes ends up as a meal for the female.

The curious courtship of scorpions has interested and intrigued many scientists. One of the most famous of these was the French naturalist Jean Henri Fabré, who lived from 1823 until 1915. He devoted many years of his long life to watching, investigating, and writing about insects, spiders, and scorpions. His detailed descriptions of their habits are read widely even today.

Scorpion courtship dance.

During their display, the paired scorpions seek a smooth surface for themselves. They bring their mouth parts close to each other as though to kiss. Then the two jerk their bodies to and fro without moving their legs.

In the next part of their ritual, male and female curve their tails forward high over their backs, and may touch and even entwine them. Then, they appear to fight each other.

For many years no one knew how the male scorpion fertilized the female's eggs. In 1956, a woman scientist discovered that the male gives off his sperm in a small packet or *spermatophore*. He glues this to the ground and then tries to lead the female to it. Walking back and forth, over and over again, the female finally locates the sperm packet with her genital opening.

5

Birth of Young

The female scorpion carries her eggs for a few months to one year. Her abdomen swells as the eggs develop inside her body. At birth, she forms a basket with her legs to catch her young as they emerge. Each is inside a thin, white sac which soon breaks open. The white, soft-shelled newborns climb on their mother's back. Often, the mother is nearly hidden from view by her piggyback babies of which there may be dozens.

The mother scorpion does not feed her youngsters. They do not need to eat immediately because their plump, quarter-inch-long bodies contain yolk for nourishment.

After the first molt occurs in one or two weeks, the young look more like typical scorpions, except for their smaller size. They stay with their mother for a day or so

Female Diplocentrus peloncillensis *with young on her back.*

more and then go their separate ways to fend for themselves.

The mother scorpion soon loses any maternal instinct
she has and, if her babies wander back, she may attack and
eat her own offspring.

30

Juvenile Diplocentrus peloncillensis.

Scorpions usually molt seven or eight times before they are fully grown. Typically, several years pass before maturity is reached.

6

Eating and Being Eaten

Scorpions eat many kinds of living things. It is still some-
what of a mystery how they detect their prey. The fine
sensory hairs on their pedipalps and exoskeletons are
thought to play a key role. In their diets are adult and
larval insects such as cockroaches, beetles, and crickets.
They also eat centipedes, millipedes, and even small lizards
and rodents. Many spiders, including large tarantulas, are
fed upon as well.

When a scorpion is resting, its underside touches the
ground, legs are folded, and the tail is curved up or curled
to one side. But if a hungry scorpion senses prey, it rises
up on its legs and moves forward, looking like a wrestler
with its fearsomely large claws out front and open. Now

Encounter between tarantula and scorpion.

A roadrunner—predator of the scorpion.

its treacherous tail is arched overhead, anticipating action.

The scorpion swiftly snatches its victim with its pedipalps and stings without delay. The pedipalps carry the meal toward the pincers where it is torn apart. Finally, the pincers push the pieces into the hair-lined mouth where digestive juices turn them into a soft pulp or liquid which the scorpion then sucks in. Any hard leftover bits are simply tossed away.

Eating is a slow process for scorpions and a large meal

may take hours to finish. As long as food is available, a scorpion eats regularly. But once an adult scorpion is well fed, it can live for months without food if need be.

Wherever they live in the world, scorpions have natural enemies. Among these are several birds. In our Southwest, adult elf owls, which are only about the size of a sparrow, often eat scorpions and also feed them to their young. The parent birds neatly clip off the stingers before giving the scorpions to their nestlings. Roadrunners also eat many scorpions.

Centipedes, ground beetles, mantids, spiders, bats, and lizards all prey upon scorpions successfully, at least part of the time.

Not to be forgotten is that scorpions kill and eat many of their own kind.

7

Some Common Scorpions of the United States

Some of our scorpions are encountered more often than others. Members of the family Buthidae are well known, especially those of the genus *Centruroides*. As a group, these are called bark scorpions because they frequently are found under the loose bark of trees.

The common stripe-back scorpion lives throughout our southern states, and westward into New Mexico. It is a pale scorpion, about two and one-half inches long, with two dark stripes on its back.

Two scorpions found in Florida are the brown and Hentz's *Centruroides*. The first is nearly three inches in length and a uniform dark reddish brown or nearly black.

A brown Centruroides (C. gracilis) *with young.*

The smaller Hentz's has a lighter background color with mottled legs and dark stripes on its back.

The deadly sculptured scorpion is thought to live entirely within the state of Arizona. It is a yellowish, straw color and has no stripes. However, there is a less numerous

Giant hairy scorpion.

striped variety of the sculptured scorpion, also found only in Arizona, which used to be thought of as a separate species. Both of these are slender appearing and usually measure two to three inches.

Within the Vejovid family are our largest scorpions, the giant hairy scorpions. These are members of the genus *Hadrurus*. They live throughout the Southwest and grow to well over six inches long. They have abundant sensory hairs on their yellow to greenish-yellow bodies, hence their names.

Stripe-tail devil scorpion.

The northern scorpion has been seen from Nebraska to Idaho, in Utah, Nevada, the Badlands of North Dakota, and as far north as Alberta, Canada. Its two-inch body is yellowish green.

In Texas, Arizona, and California are stripe-tail devil scorpions. These are two to three inches in length and a greenish-yellow color. Their name describes the four dark lines on the underside of the tail.

From South Carolina to Texas live southern unstriped devil scorpions. These have patterned backs and are a dark reddish brown.

The Pacific Coast scorpion lives in California and Ore-

Pacific Coast scorpion.

gon. It is two and one-half inches long and dark brown with pale legs. Southern California is also home for the shiny-stinged scorpion, which is reddish brown with black pedipalps. This scorpion burrows into the ground and waits for an unsuspecting insect to pass by the entrance of its tunnel.

Only a few scorpions of the family Diplocentridae have been reported in the United States. They are all of the genus *Diplocentrus* and have been seen in Florida, Texas, New Mexico, and California.

Many other kinds of scorpions live in the United States, but they are fewer in number and so less likely to be seen.

8

The Sting

When a scorpion stings, it whips its tail forward, curving it over its head. The sharp stinger thrusts into its victim, oftentimes repeatedly. With each piercing of the prey, venom is left behind. As the stinger is pulled out, the wound closes around the poison so that it cannot leak out.

A scorpion sting from a nondeadly species produces a burning sensation at the site of the wound. The immediate area may become swollen and discolored. A blister often forms where the stinger pricked the skin. Effects usually last for eight to twelve hours.

Although most scorpion stings are not serious, the United States Public Health Service cautions that *all* scorpion stings should be seen by a medical doctor as soon as

A stinger of a giant hairy scorpion.

possible. Even if a sting is from a scorpion which is thought to be harmless, there is a chance of developing infections.

The most dangerous scorpion in the United States is the sculptured scorpion of Arizona. Its poison, like that of other lethal species of the world, produces alarming effects because it attacks the nervous system of its victim.

42

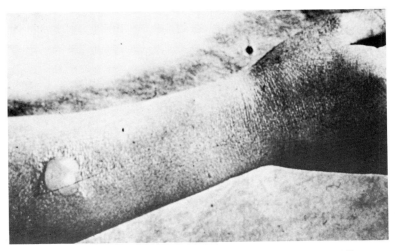

The site of a scorpion sting on a human arm. Note the blister.

A deadly sting at first results in a prickly-pin sensation at the site of the sting. The spot may become painful. If the sting is on a hand or foot, these feelings and a strange numbness travel up the arm or leg toward the body. Swelling and discoloration normally do not occur at the site of the wound when a deadly species is involved. Untreated, the effects increase.

For people who have recovered from the sting of the sculptured scorpion, the last spot on the body to heal is the original site of the sting.

The deadly sculptured scorpion.

Immediate first aid for someone stung by a scorpion can be vital. The United States Public Health Service advises that it is important to chill the wound and surrounding area quickly with crushed ice packs or ice water. This slows down the spread of venom while the patient is being brought to a physician. Whenever possible, the scorpion

44

which has stung a person should be saved for positive identification.

In our country, an antivenom (anti- means against) is available to treat stings of the sculptured scorpion. This was developed at the Poisonous Animals Research Laboratory at Arizona State University and is distributed to storage depots around the state.

A person who discovers a scorpion on himself should brush it off rather than try to swat it to lessen the chance of being stung.

Many kinds of scorpions hide under loose bark, old logs, rocks, boards, and other similar moist dark places. In areas where scorpions are plentiful, objects on the ground should be picked up with caution because scorpions tend to cling to the undersides. Also, it is best not to walk barefoot outside after dark, since scorpions are most active then.

In regions where scorpions may enter houses, people should check their shoes, clothing, and bedding before using them. A row of smoothly finished glazed tiles cemented to the outside walls of a house just above the ground acts as a barrier to scorpions.

Cats can be trained to catch scorpions and seem to be quite unaffected by their venom. Their fur and natural mousing habits also tend to keep them from being stung.

Scorpions fluoresce or glow in the dark when viewed with ultraviolet light. Such a light is helpful to detect scorpions and often is used by scientists to collect the animals for study.

Perhaps the best scorpion control is to clear away unnecessary piles of lumber, boxes, rags, and other items which are hiding places where scorpions easily find insects to eat and can breed.

Few chemicals have been found which are effective in repelling scorpions while still being safe for the environment.

Even though scorpions are not creatures we want to come in contact with, they fill a role in nature as food for other animals and as predators. They have survived nearly unchanged since before the age of dinosaurs to the present day. Scientists believe there is still much to learn about these unusual and fascinating animals.

Common and Scientific Names
of U.S. Scorpions in the Text

Family Buthidae:

Brown *Centruroides*	*Centruroides gracilis*
Sculptured Scorpion	*Centruroides sculpturatus*
Common Stripe-back	
Scorpion	*Centruroides vittatus*
Hentz's *Centruroides*	*Centruroides hentzi*

Family Vejovidae:

Pacific Coast Scorpion	*Uroctonus mordax*
Shiny-stinged Scorpion	*Anuroctonus phaiodactylus*
Northern Scorpion	*Vejovis boreus*
Stripe-tail Devil Scorpion	*Vejovis spinigerus*
Southern Unstriped	
Devil Scorpion	*Vejovis carolinianus*
Giant Hairy Scorpions	*Hadrurus* sp.

Family Diplocentridae:

Only one genus of this family is represented in the United States, *Diplocentrus*.

Index

J 595.4 B
BILLINGS, CHARLENE W.
SCORPIONS

45255

DISCARD